SCHOOL START STORYBOOKS: BOZO THE CLOWN

In this beautifully illustrated storybook, part of the *School Start* series, children with language needs can explore the story of Bozo the Clown as he tries to make a new friend.

School Start Storybooks support language development in reception and Key Stage 1 aged children both in school and at home. Through beautifully illustrated stories, children are invited to explore language, ask questions and recall events in order to aid language development, listening and memory skills. Each book contains a colourful and engaging story designed to appeal to young children, and with language specifically chosen for children with language needs.

Key skills that these books support include:

- Comprehension
- Expression
- Vocabulary
- Memory
- Sequencing

Available either as a set or as individual books, the *School Start Storybooks* are a vital resource for professionals looking to support language development either with individual children, or groups of children. Each book also contains guidance and prompt questions to help the supporting adult use the book effectively, making it ideal for parents to support language development at home.

Catherine de la Bedoyere is a speech and language therapist with over 25 years' experience of working with children, including managing and delivering services in a variety of early years and school settings.

Liam de la Bedoyere is an illustrator and designer.

T0002675

School Start

School Start is a series of practical resources to be used with children who need additional help in developing communication skills.

Pre-School Start: Targeted Intervention for Language Ages 3 and 4 (Reception–1)
PB: 978-1-90930-175-7

School Start: Targeted Intervention for Language and Sound Awareness in Reception Class (2nd edition)
PB: 978-1-90939-158-0

School Start Year 1: Targeted Intervention for Language and Sound Awareness
PB: 978-1-13857-395-6

School Start Storybooks: Supporting Auditory Memory and Sequencing Skills in Key Stage 1 (Available as a set or as individual books)
PB: 978-1-138-34283-5

School Start Storybooks: Bozo the Clown
PB: 978-0-367-81017-7

School Start Storybooks: Nik the Ninja
PB: 978-0-367-40971-5

School Start Storybooks: Rusty the Robber
PB: 978-0-367-40972-2

School Start Storybooks

Bozo the Clown

Catherine de la Bedoyere

Liam de la Bedoyere

Routledge
Taylor & Francis Group

LONDON AND NEW YORK

First published 2020
by Routledge
2 Park Square, Milton Park, Abingdon, Oxon OX14 4RN

and by Routledge
52 Vanderbilt Avenue, New York, NY 10017

Routledge is an imprint of the Taylor & Francis Group, an informa business

© 2020 Catherine de la Bedoyere
Illustrations © 2020 by Liam de la Bedoyere

The right of Catherine de la Bedoyere to be identified as author of this work and Liam de la Bedoyere to be identified as illustrator of this work has been asserted by them in accordance with sections 77 and 78 of the Copyright, Designs and Patents Act 1988.

All rights reserved. No part of this book may be reprinted or reproduced or utilised in any form or by any electronic, mechanical, or other means, now known or hereafter invented, including photocopying and recording, or in any information storage or retrieval system, without permission in writing from the publishers.

Trademark notice: Product or corporate names may be trademarks or registered trademarks, and are used only for identification and explanation without intent to infringe.

British Library Cataloguing-in-Publication Data
A catalogue record for this book is available from the British Library

Library of Congress Cataloging-in-Publication Data
A catalog record for this book has been requested

ISBN: 978-0-367-81017-7 (pbk)
ISBN: 978-0-367-81018-4 (ebk)

Typeset in Calibri
by Apex CoVantage, LLC

School Start Storybooks support language development in children aged 5–7 at school and home. The books present stories that appeal to this age group, are adjusted for children with language needs and provide guides for the adult reader to help with:

Comprehension ☐

Expression ☐

Vocabulary ☐

Memory ☐

Sequencing ☐

'As a speech and language therapist, I find that sharing stories is an excellent way of introducing children with language needs to new language forms. By reading aloud picture books to children, we can explore new words, ask questions that prompt discussion and recall what has happened. However, it can be hard to find books that both interest this age group that are written in differentiated language. So I have created stories that are designed to be read aloud by an adult to a child, or group of children. I often talk to teaching assistants in schools about using spoken stories for language, as oppose to learning to read. They usually ask me how to ask questions, which words to talk about and how to demonstrate meaning; for this reason, I have included prompts and directions for adults throughout the text.' Catherine de la Bedoyere

Bozo the Clown also features in *School Start Year 1* Sound Awareness programme (2019) and it may be read alongside this group programme.

Instructions

Please read this story aloud to a child or group of children. Hold the book so that you can read the text and the children can see the illustration. Prompts to develop language are embedded in the text (see below). Do not deliver all the prompts and questions in the first reading; aim to introduce more on each re-reading of the story. Above all, please remember that sharing books is supposed to be a fun and interactive experience for children and adults alike.

Animated voice and expressions!

Children with limited language rely on tone of voice, gesture and facial expression to help them decode the meaning of words. We typically use this exaggeration with under fives, but children over five with limited language still benefit from your acting talents.

! will give you a prompt to add a little emphasis.

Miming and pointing

To help children understand the words in the story, mime the actions and point to the relevant illustrations. Children with limited language tend to be visual learners and will bootstrap their visual understanding to their verbal understanding if you provide this support.

Prompts to mime and point are printed in italics in the text.

Vocabulary

The text will introduce a variety of new words and word forms to children with plenty of repetition to aid learning. Children with difficulty learning and remembering new words need many more opportunities to hear the word in context than typically developing children. Reading the story many times gives multiple opportunities, but even better will be hearing the word in everyday use. Each time you read the book, focus on different words in the text and try to use the word in real life during that day, e.g. feelings such as happy and sad.

To focus on a word when reading the story:

* Say it clearly, stop and repeat it

* Encourage the children to ask you what it means

* Show what it means, e.g. point to Bozo the Clown

* Use gesture, e.g. say 'first' as you hold up one finger and 'next' as you hold up a second finger

* Suggest or compare a word or phrase with a similar meaning, e.g. cops/police, shake/tremble, nervous/scared

* Compare the word with the opposite meaning, e.g. heavy/light, happy/sad

* Compare different forms of the same word, e.g. catch/caught, leap/leapt, fly/flew, throw/threw

* In this book, emphasis is given to forms of dialogue (said, replied, yelled etc.) and ways of feeling (sad, shy, brave etc.); the many examples give you the opportunity to draw the children's attention to how words express meaning

Suggested vocabulary to teach is printed in **bold**.

Questions

Suggested questions are inserted into the story as a prompt for you.

Allow the children time to give you an answer. Children with limited language typically find the closed questions about something visual or concrete easier to answer, e.g. 'Do you get pocket money, Yes? No?' but may still need you to model alternative answers. Harder questions expect the child to relate the story to their own experience, e.g. 'Did you do something kind today?' Pause to give the children time to answer, but be ready to suggest or model an answer to scaffold their attempt to respond, e.g. 'Sometimes children are kind when they share their book in class', etc. Questions are used in the book to demonstrate how to understand and answer different question forms, as well as engaging children in the story as active listeners. They are not there to 'test' but to 'teach and engage'.

Questions are indicated in the text by colour and 'Q:'

Question prompt cards available in *School Start Year 1* may be used to aid understanding of the different question forms.

Memory: lists and information recall

To encourage active listening and develop short-term memory, play a question game with the children that will require them to recall what they have seen and discussed on that page.

At the end of the page, turn the book so the children cannot see the illustrations. Ask them the prompt questions so that they recall items as a group. Use the illustrations to confirm or prompt responses once the children have had a go at answering.

Memory: sequencing

Children learning and remembering verbal language are helped if they have a story structure that provides a frame; for instance what happened, first, next and last? This is why it can be so helpful to teach children a) sequencing terms ('first, next, last' or 'beginning, middle, end') and b) how to recall events in a sequence. As the child learns these foundation skills, it will become easier for them to understand the information given in the classroom. Stories are the natural place to develop sequencing skills. For this reason, the text frequently uses sequencing terms, such as 'finally'.

At the end of the story, there are prompt questions to recap the story sequence. Use the illustrations to confirm or prompt responses once the children have had a go at answering.

Sharing the story at home

Sit with your child so they can see the pictures.

Read the story to your child, pointing to the pictures to help them understand.

Use your acting skills (face and voice) to bring the words to life.

Next time you read the story, ask some of the questions. Pause to give your child time to answer; but if they struggle, tell them the answer.

Each time you read the story, ask more questions and stop to explain what a word (**in bold**) means.

Try and use new words at other times in the day to help your child become confident with the word.

Do not expect your child to read the written words; this is a listening activity, not a reading activity.

Stop if your child loses focus ☐

Sharing stories is fun ☐

Build on success ☐

Teach don't test ☐

Why this book may help your child at home

In class, children are expected to listen to the teacher, understand the information and follow instructions. To be successful at this, the children must be able to pay attention, listen, understand the words and grammar and finally remember what has been said in the right order. For some children, these skills are slower to develop than for others and typically these children will struggle in class. There are many ways to help such children but sharing stories can be one of the most enjoyable and simple activities to boost listening and language.

During infant school years, teaching places focus on children becoming readers. Reading will introduce children to more formal and complex language than they will hear in the playground and so it is an important part of child language development. Children who are having trouble with spoken language are likely to find learning to read and understand written words difficult. So for these children, it is important to continue to read stories aloud to them until they can read independently; this will make sure they are not missing out on the opportunity to extend their language experience.

Once upon a time, there was a clown called Bozo. Here is a picture of Bozo. *(Point to the illustration.)*

Bozo is a circus clown and he does tricks at Merryville **fairground** to entertain children. He is very good at riding the unicycle. He can even ride his unicycle and hold a jelly at the same time!

Q: Do you know what a unicycle is? It's a bike with just one wheel; isn't he clever at balancing?

Q: Can you balance standing on just one leg? *(Ask the children to try.)*

And here is Spud the Clown Dog. He does tricks too. *(Point to the illustration.)*

Bozo is a fantastic clown but he is very shy. He wants to find a friend but he is scared to say 'Hello' to people! Having no friends makes him feel sad and lonely.

Memory Questions:

Q: What is Bozo riding?

Q: What is Bozo holding?

Bozo really wants to be friends with Elsa.

Here is Elsa. Elsa sells ice cream from her ice cream van at the fairground.

'I think Elsa will be my friend because she likes clowns. Look there is a red clown nose on her ice cream van,' he said.

Q: Have you got a friend? Why do you like them?

'How can I get Elsa to notice me and be my friend?' Bozo asked. 'I have an idea! I will show her I am brave, strong, clever and **COOL** at the fairground stalls. Then she will want to be my friend.'

Memory Question:

Q: What has Elsa got on the front of her ice cream van?

'I know, I will show Elsa how **brave** I am at the **circus** stall.' Bozo went over to the circus stall, where he listened to the loud ringmaster shouting 'Roll up, roll up. Who is brave enough to perform the Ring of Fire Challenge?'

'I am!' yelled Bozo.

'Good man,' answered the ringmaster. 'All you have to do is jump through this Ring of Fire!'

Bozo jumped up on the stage looking very pleased with himself. 'This will **impress** Elsa,' he said. So he looked over to where Elsa was in the ice cream van to see if she was watching him.

But when Bozo got up close to the fire it was very hot and Bozo got **scared**. Bozo started to **shake** and **tremble** with **fear**, he stepped back and fell into a bucket of water!

Poor Bozo. Elsa didn't think Bozo was brave at jumping through fire! She thought he was very funny and she started to laugh.

Q: Do you think it is dangerous to jump through the Ring of Fire? Why? What could go wrong?

Memory Question:

Q: What has Elsa got on the front of her ice cream van?

'Oh dear, Elsa doesn't think I'm brave. But maybe I can show her I am **strong**?' thought Bozo as he went over to the strongman stall.

Bozo secretly watched the strongman lift the heavy **hammer** and hit the machine. The ball **flew** up to the top and rang the bell! *(Point to the illustration to show the movement.)* 'DING, DING, DING,' sounded the bell. And the children watching called out, 'WOW!' *(Point to the illustration.)*

'I can do that,' Bozo **boasted**. So, he puffed out his chest to look as big and strong and possible.

Then he looked over at Elsa to make sure she was watching. 'I'm going to hit the top just like the strongman.'

Bozo lifted the big hammer and nearly fell over because it was so **heavy**! So instead, he picked up the **light** hammer and went 'Bang' down on the. . .

Q: What did Bozo hit?

Poor Bozo missed the machine and banged the hammer down on the strongman's foot! Elsa didn't think Bozo was strong at all! She thought he was very funny and she started to laugh. AGAIN!

Memory Question:

Q: What did Bozo use to hit the machine, the heavy hammer or the light hammer?

'Elsa doesn't think I am brave or strong. So I will show Elsa how **clever** I am instead. I will show her I can juggle,' said Bozo.

At the juggling stall, there was a big bear juggling and wobbling on a red ball. 'May I have a turn?' Bozo shouted. 'I'm really good at juggling and **balancing**.'

The big bear growled, 'No Bozo, YOU can't juggle.'

Q: Is the bear being rude or kind?

'Oh yes, I can juggle if you give me a chance!' Bozo **argued**. So the bear threw three red balls to Bozo.

Bozo looked over to make sure Elsa was watching. But he was so **nervous** that his hands were **hot** and **sweaty**. So when he picked up the red juggling balls and tossed them in the air, WHOOPS! Down they all fell.

Poor Bozo. Elsa didn't think Bozo was clever at juggling! She thought he was very funny and she carried on laughing.

Q: Can you juggle? *(Give the children soft balls or beanbags so they can try juggling.)*

Memory Questions:

Q: Did Bozo juggle the red or blue balls?

Q: How many balls did the big bear throw to Bozo?

'Maybe I can show Elsa how Cool I am because I can shoot arrows and hit the target,' thought Bozo, and he ran over to the **archery** stall.

Here is a picture of the archery stall with the target, bows and arrows. *(Point to the illustration.)*

Bozo greeted the archer, 'Hello there!' He asked, 'How do I hit the **target**?' The archer picked up the **bow** and **arrow**, then showed Bozo how to shoot at the target. *(Act out using a bow and arrow.)*

'That looks **easy**!' said Bozo. 'No, it isn't,' answered the archer and he gave Bozo the bow and arrow to try.

Q: Do you think Bozo will hit the bull's eye when he has a turn?

First Bozo looked over to Elsa to make sure she was watching. Then he took aim and fired. But the arrow went 'WOOSH' and hit a little girl's balloon. It burst! The little girl cried, 'Waa! Waa!'

Poor Bozo. Elsa didn't think Bozo was cool at shooting arrows! She thought he was very funny though and laughed some more.

Memory Question:

Q: What did Bozo hit with his arrow?

Bozo was sad thinking about how he had messed up. 'Now Elsa doesn't think I am brave, or strong, or clever, or cool,' he whimpered. 'Maybe I can give her a present instead,' and he went over to the balloon stall to make a balloon to give Elsa.

First, he watched the stallholder **blow** up a yellow balloon and **fold** it into a balloon-dog. 'That looks like my sort of trick,' said Bozo. 'May I have a go?' he asked.

Q: What kind of balloon would you make? A dog? A star? A moon?

'Here you go,' offered the stallholder as he gave Bozo a fresh, yellow balloon. Bozo started to **twist** and **shape** the **squeaky**, **slippery** balloon. *(Act folding and twisting. You can use a tea towel to demonstrate and take turns.)*

But just then he heard someone shouting!

Memory Question:

Q: What colour is the balloon-dog?

'HELP! HELP!' cried Elsa. 'Spud the Clown Dog is stealing my ice cream!'

The **greedy** dog jumped out of Elsa's ice cream van with a big, mint ice cream in his mouth.

'Someone call the cops, 999!' **yelled** Elsa. 'That naughty dog has to be stopped!'

'Aha, the perfect moment for me to be a **hero,**' thought Bozo. 'I can show her I am brave, strong, clever and cool if I can catch Spud the Clown Dog!'

'Never fear, Bozo's here!' shouted Bozo to Elsa. 'Super-Clown Bozo to the **rescue**. No need for the cops.' And with that, Bozo hopped onto his unicycle to chase Spud the Clown Dog.

Memory Questions:

Q: What flavour ice cream was the dog eating?

Q: What number is it to call the cops?

Bozo **pedalled** *(act out)* as fast as his legs would go, chasing Spud through the fairground. But Spud was **quick** and **darted** in and out of all the stalls. Bozo could not catch Spud the Clown Dog.

First, Spud ran to the balloon stall and grabbed Bozo's balloon with his sharp teeth. POP! And the balloon was burst!

'How clever Spud is,' said Elsa.

Next, Spud jumped through the Ring of Fire at the circus stall.

'How brave Spud is,' said Elsa.

Memory Questions:

Q: Where did Spud go first?

Q: Where did Spud go next?
(Look back at previous illustrations to check and prompt answers.)

Then, Spud ran over to the archery stall; with one big jump, he **leapt** into the air and caught an arrow in his mouth! He looked like he was grinning! *(Point to the illustration.)*

Next, Spud ran over to the strongman stall. He jumped high in the air and landed right on top of the strongman machine. 'DING, DING, DING,' rang the bell.

'What a strong dog Spud is!' said Elsa.

'What a cool and **cheeky** dog Spud is!' said Elsa.

Memory Questions:

Q: Where did Spud find the arrow? At the … stall

Q: Where did Spud ring the bell? At the … stall

'I know that sound,' shouted Bozo when he heard the bell. 'I know where Spud is now!' Bozo cycled to the strongman stall as fast as possible. He hopped off his unicycle and caught that naughty dog in his arms.

'Now Elsa will think I am brave and strong and clever because I **caught** Spud the Clown Dog,' thought Bozo, 'and she will want to be my friend.'

Bozo carried Spud to Elsa's ice-cream van and put Spud on the ground. But poor Bozo, Elsa was laughing again!

'Why are you laughing?' asked Bozo.

'Because you are the **funniest** clown in the world and I like you just as you are!' Elsa declared. 'You really make me **happy**. Will you be my friend?'

Memory Questions:

Q: Why does Elsa want Bozo to be her friend?

Q: What is in Bozo's hair?

'Now what are we going to do with you?' asked Elsa, looking at Spud the Clown Dog. 'It is very naughty to steal my ice-cream.' Spud sat on the ground **grinning** at Elsa.

The circus ringmaster came over. 'Right then, right then,' he said. 'What have we got here? A Clown Dog that steals ice cream! I think we had better take you down to the police station, you naughty dog.' And he wagged his finger at Spud.

'No, no,' cried Elsa 'I have a much better idea.'

Memory Question:

Q: What did Spud steal from Elsa?
(Look back at the previous illustration to check and prompt an answer.)

'Everyone comes to Merryville fairground to have a good time, to laugh and make friends,' said Elsa. 'Bozo and Spud can make us all happy by doing clown tricks for us!'

So, she gave Bozo three mint ice creams to juggle. Bozo hopped up on his unicycle and started to juggle.

'Hurrah!' shouted all the children.

Then Spud jumped up and grabbed an ice cream and balanced it on his nose! Clever dog!

Everyone laughed, including Bozo and Elsa, who were now best friends.

'All's well that ends well,' sighed the ringmaster.

The End.

Q: Do you think Elsa and Bozo will stay friends?

Q: How do you keep your friends?

Memory: sequence

Q: What happened at the beginning of the story?

Prompt using illustrations of Bozo on his unicycle and Elsa in her van.

Q: What happened in the middle of the story?

Prompt using illustrations of Bozo visiting stalls and chasing Spud.

Q: What happened at the end of the story?

Prompt using illustrations of Bozo juggling ice cream and spud stealing ice cream.

Note: when re-reading the story, you can introduce alternative sequencing terms: 'First, next, last,' e.g. 'What happened next, and next, etc.?'